STRONGEST AND weakest

Written by
Camilla de la Bédoyère

QED

QED Publishing

Designed and edited by Starry Dog Books Ltd
Picture research: Starry Dog Books Ltd

Consultant: Dr Gerald Legg,
Booth Museum of Natural History,
Brighton

First published in the UK in 2010 by
QED Publishing
A Quarto Group company
226 City Road
London EC1V 2TT

www.qed-publishing.co.uk

A catalogue record for this book is available from
the British Library.

ISBN 978 1 84835 490 6

Printed in China

Picture credits
Key: t = top, b = bottom, l = left, r = right, c = centre,
FC = front cover, BC = back cover.

A = Alamy, BSP = Big Stock Photo.com, C = Corbis,
D = Dreamstime.com, F = Fotolibra.com,
FLPA = Frank Lane Picture Agency, G = Getty Images,
ISP = iStockphoto.com, M = Morguefile.com,
NPL = Nature Picture Library (naturepl.com),
PL = Photolibrary, PS = Photoshot,
S = Shutterstock.com, SPL = Science Photo Library.

FC l S/ © Four Oaks, FC r S/ © Pakhnyushcha;
BC l, tc, r S/ © Picsfive, BC c S/ © Neale Cousland.

1 S/ © Graeme Shannon; 2 S/ © Dennis Donohue;
3t S/ © greatpapa; 4 Wikipedia © Silke Baron;
5t IQM/ © Chris Parks, 5b S/ © Colette3; 6bl S/ ©
ZTS, 6bc IQM/ © Johnny Jensen, 6-7 S/ © Dennis
Donohue, 7tr PL (OSF)/ © Ariadne Van Zandbergen;
8 S/ © Teguh Tirtaputra; 9t PL/ © Gustav W
Verderber, 9b PL (OSF)/ © Densey Clyne; 10c S/
© Mogens Trolle, 10b PL/ © Nigel Pavitt; 11tr S/ ©
worldswildlifewonders, 11b A/ © Juniors Bildarchiv;
12 A/ © A & J Visage; 13r D/ © Ryszard, 13b D/
© Inventori; 14bl © S/ M Reel, 14-15t PL/ © Ken
Preston-Mafham, 14-15b PL/ © Nigel Dennis, 15c ©
S/ greatpapa; 16t D/ © Murielkerr, 16b S/ © Graeme
Shannon; 17 PL/ © Mauricio-Jose Schwarz; 18 NPL/
© Fred Olivier, 18-19 S/ © Gentoo Multimedia Ltd,
19t PL/ © Glenn Bartley, 19b S/ © Gentoo Multimedia
Ltd; 20 IQM/ © Dray van Beeck; 21t NPL/ © Delpho
/ ARCO, 21b SPL/ © Nicholas Smythe; 22 PL/ ©
Paul Franklin; 23t NPL/ © Peggy Stap, 23b PL/ ©
Carol Farneti Foster; 24 S/ © Eric Isselée; 25tl A/ ©
Redmond Durrell, 25tr PL/ © Chris Catton, 25b PL/
© Raymond Mendez; 26c S/ © Jeff Grabert, 26b D/ ©
Lifesazoo; 27t PL/ © Alfred & Annaliese Trunk, 27b
S/ © Eric Isselée; 28t S/ © Fred Kamphues, 28b PL/
© Cornelia Doerr; 29t S/ © 2265524729, 29b S/ ©
Stéphane Bidouze; 32 D/ © Lifesazoo.

The words
in **bold** are
explained in
the Glossary
on page 30.

Contents

Strong to Survive

Strong animals are more likely to win the battle for survival than weak ones.

Strength is about power, and being able to do something that a weak animal cannot. Strong animals, for example, might be able to lift heavy loads, defend themselves from an attacker or undertake long and dangerous journeys.

Knockout!

Mantis shrimps can deliver a deadly punch with their forelegs. The shrimps use their strength to kill snails, crabs and oysters for food. A punch from a mantis shrimp hits its target with the force of a rifle bullet.

⇐ The peacock mantis shrimp uses its club-shaped forelegs to lash out at prey at a speed of 240 metres a second.

Jelly weaklings

Comb jellies and mantis shrimps both live in the sea, but that is where their similarity ends. Graceful comb jellies could qualify as the world's weakest animals. They are too weak to move against an **ocean current**, so they spend their lives just drifting along.

⇨ *Comb jellies have little hairs, called cilia, that they beat to try and move through water. As the cilia beat, they produce beautiful colours.*

The no. 1 biggest, strongest bear **RECORD BREAKER** is the ...

POLAR BEAR

Polar bears are the biggest and strongest of all bears. They need to be strong to survive in the cold **Arctic** regions. In spring, however, polar bears are weaklings. They emerge from **hibernation** hungry and dangerous.

Strong Body

Some animals are clearly built for strength.

Strong animals have bodies that are tough or powerful. The strongest animals can drag or lift things heavier than themselves.

Bones and muscles

Many animals have bony skeletons. A skeleton supports a body and provides a perfect framework for muscles to work against. Muscles are attached to bones, and they can pull against them to get more power and strength.

⇨ Pumas are big cats with great strength and speed. They leap onto their prey to catch it, and can run holding an animal as big as a deer in their mouth.

6

ACTUAL ≪ SIZE ≫

Vertebrates are animals with backbones. The smallest vertebrates in the world are tiny fish called dwarf gobies. The bones and muscles of these little fish give them the strength to swim.

Dwarf goby

8 7 6 5 4 3 2 1
cm

Tough shells

Crabs are **crustaceans**. They have a strong outer shell called a carapace. The carapace is made of a tough **mineral** called calcium carbonate. It protects the crab's delicate organs, such as its gills, which it uses to breathe. A crab's large claws are powerful weapons. It uses them to scare away rivals, as well as to pinch, crush and pick up food.

⇧ *A robber, or coconut, crab is strong enough to haul itself up a tree and grab a coconut, which it cracks open with its giant claws.*

Weak Will Do

Not all animals rely on strength to survive. Some prefer to use poison.

Some animals contain a poison that injures or kills predators who try to eat them. Other animals deliver venom by stinging, stabbing or biting.

⇩ *One bite from a blue-ringed octopus can kill a human in just four minutes.*

Ring of death

The blue-ringed octopus has a soft, boneless body and measures just 10 to 20 centimetres long. Yet this weakling bites to kill.

The blue-ringed octopus makes two types of venom in its mouth – a mild one that it uses for prey such as crabs, and a stronger one used in defence. The octopus wraps its tentacles around an attacker and bites, injecting its deadly venom.

↑ Deathstalker scorpion

Deathstalker scorpions live in North Africa and the Middle East. They are only 10 centimetres long, but the venom contained in the stinger at the end of their tail can kill animals much larger than themselves.

Spider poison

Spiders don't look like tough animals, but most of them have venom that they use to kill insects. Male Sydney funnel-web spiders are one of the world's deadliest spiders. They lunge their enormous fangs into an attacker and inject a fast-acting poison that is deadly to humans and monkeys.

9

↑ A male Sydney funnel-web spider rears up, ready to strike. Females also have venom, but it is not so deadly.

Victims of the Hunt

During a hunt, the strongest and weakest animals battle it out for survival.

Predators are animals that hunt other animals for food. They usually seek out weak or injured animals, because they are easier targets. Animals that predators attack are called prey.

⇧ *Young lions hunt with the lionesses and learn from them.*

Powerful pride

Big cats are among the strongest of all predators. Most big cats hunt alone, but lions live in a group called a pride, and they often hunt as a pack. They prey on grazing animals, such as antelopes.

ACTUAL «« SIZE »»

Lions have enormous fangs, or canine teeth. These tough teeth are pointed and sharp – perfect for stabbing prey and inflicting fatal wounds. Male lions also use their fangs when they fight one another.

Lion's canine tooth

Speed is strength

The lions identify a young or weak member of the antelope herd and circle it. When they launch an attack, the antelope's best defense is speed. If the lionsare successful, they will pull the prey down to the ground with their mouth and clawed paws.

⇐This lioness puts on a burst of speed before pouncing to catch a bird.

Carry that Load

Many strong animals can carry heavy weights.

Predators often carry their food to a place where they can eat it without being disturbed.

⇩ *A wolverine has incredibly powerful jaws and tough teeth. It will have no trouble crunching and chewing this bone from a much larger animal.*

Brave and bold

Wolverines are no bigger than a dog, but they are regarded as one of the strongest **mammals** alive. These bearlike creatures are so strong that they can pull open a steel trap and drag a dead animal that is much heavier than themselves for several kilometres. Wolverines are so sure of their strength that they will fight bears and pumas for food.

Mighty ants

Leafcutter ants use their sharp jaws for slicing through leaves. The biggest and strongest ants carry fragments of leaves back to their nest. The bits of leaf are used to feed a **fungus** in the nest that the ants eat.

⇨ *A group of leafcutter ants marches back to the nest with a piece of leaf. One ant stands on the leaf to guard the workers from attackers.*

13

ACTUAL «« SIZE »»

The rhinoceros beetle is one of the strongest animals in the world. It could carry a load up to 850 times its own weight on its back. In fact, these beetles have no reason to carry anything so heavy, but being so strong makes them less likely to get crushed.

Rhinoceros beetle

1 cm 2 3 4 5 6 7 8 9 10 11 12

Armour Plated

Weaklings can make themselves tough with super-strong skin.

Some animals protect the soft, delicate organs inside their body by having scales, tough bony plates or spines on their outside.

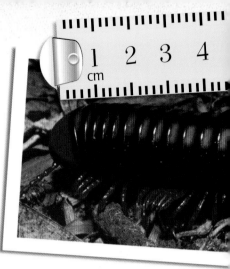

The no. 1 longest-living **RECORD BREAKER** is the ...

GALAPAGOS GIANT TORTOISE

The Galapagos giant tortoise is an armour-plated monster that grows to 120 centimetres long. One of these tortoises, named Harriet, lived to be 176 years old and was the longest-living land animal ever known.

Peculiar pangolins

Pangolins, or scaly anteaters, are mammals with razor-sharp, overlapping scales covering most of their body. When attacked by a larger animal, such as a leopard or hyena, they can roll up into a ball, so no soft parts are exposed to the predator's teeth or claws.

⇩ *Pangolins have poor eyesight, and find their way using their sense of smell.*

Giant millipede

ACTUAL « SIZE »

Like pangolins, giant millipedes can roll themselves up, so only their tough outer skin is exposed. In Madagascar, lemurs roll millipedes over their bodies to release chemicals that keep flies away!

⇨ *A pufferfish swallows lots of water to make its body swell up.*

All puffed up

When a pufferfish is attacked, it makes itself look bigger and tougher than it really is. It swells its scaly body, and as it gets bigger, its spines stand up on end.

Mighty Mates

Male animals often need their strength to win the attention of a female.

Strength and size usually go hand in hand, so males are often bigger than females.

⇧ *An enormous male elephant seal lies next to a much smaller female.*

Strong to fight

When elephant seals are born, male and female **pups** are the same size, but the males grow much faster than the females. By adulthood, the males are up to 5 metres long and are five times heavier than their partners. Male elephant seals use their great strength and size to fight with one another. They also inflate their huge nose, which looks like a short trunk.

Proud as a peacock

Peacocks don't use strength to impress the females, but they do make themselves look much bigger by raising their fine feathers, or **plumage**. The females are more interested in a glorious display of colour than in watching a fight. The most attractive males get the most mates, so putting looks before muscles works for these birds.

⇩ *A peacock struts around to show off his fine feathers. The female is called a peahen. Her plumage is drab by comparison.*

Inner Strength

Penguins are not particularly powerful birds, but the adults have an inner strength.

Emperor penguins undergo a remarkable test of endurance during the **Antarctic** winter.

Freezing fathers

In March, emperor penguins walk for about 200 kilometres to their breeding grounds, where each female lays an egg. The male then balances the egg on his feet to keep it warm, and the female returns to the sea to hunt. The male looks after the egg for nine long weeks, enduring hurricane-force winds, snow and near starvation.

⬇ *A male emperor penguin guards his egg with his life. He can tuck it beneath his feathers, in an area called a brood pouch.*

The no. 1
longest journey
**RECORD
BREAKER** is the ...
SOOTY SHEARWATER

Every year, humpback whales make a return journey of 17,400 kilometres between the Antarctic and Colombia in South America. Sooty shearwaters, however, easily top this by flying for 64,000 kilometres in a single journey!

⬇ *Emperor penguin chicks are weak and vulnerable to attack by seabirds. Their parents do their best to look after them.*

Chilly chicks

When the female emperor penguins return from the sea, they look after their newly hatched chick and the males march back to the sea to feed. The chicks depend on their parents for survival. They are weak and have no way to feed themselves until they finally make their own way to the sea months later.

19

Jaws and Claws

Strength alone is rarely enough to win a battle. Specialized body parts are also often needed.

Among the tools used by animals for fighting are long teeth and hooked claws, called talons.

Grip and rip

Predators usually have specialized teeth that can tear, slice and grind their victim's flesh. Sharks grow new teeth throughout their lives, so they can replace any that break or fall out.

⇨ The American bald eagle is a bird of prey with a wingspan of about 2 metres. It is incredibly strong.

Sky hunters

Some predators, such as **birds of prey**, use long, hooked claws to grip on to wriggling prey. These enormous birds have massive wings and a curved bill that is perfect for ripping flesh. They kill other birds in flight, or swoop to grab animals off the ground or fish out of the water.

⇦ The saw-edged teeth of sandtiger sharks are perfect for killing fish. These sharks sometimes gang up to hunt their prey.

ACTUAL «« SIZE »»

Pink fairy armadillo

The pink fairy armadillo is too small and weak to fight off most predators. However, it can use its strong claws to dig a burrow when it wants to escape from danger.

1 2 3 4 5 6 7 8
cm

Parent Power

When animals are born, they are usually weak and defenceless.

Some youngsters have to make the difficult journey to adulthood alone, while others have parents that protect them.

⇩ *A male midwife toad looks after the female's eggs by keeping them moist, or they will not hatch. In dry weather, he dips them in a pond.*

Taking care

It is rare for frogs and toads to take care of their offspring. Midwife toads, however, are caring parents. The female lays her eggs and passes them to her mate. He holds them on his hind legs while they grow, then drops them into a pond when they are ready to hatch into **tadpoles**.

Snakes on guard

After a snake has laid her eggs, she may leave them to hatch on their own. However, some snakes, such as pythons, stay with their eggs to stop predators from eating them, and to keep them warm. Other snakes keep their eggs inside their body until they are ready to hatch. The mothers give birth to live young, which are stronger and more likely to survive.

⬇ Newly hatched green tree pythons are usually red or yellow. They change colour as they get older.

Strength in Numbers

Weak individuals can come together in a group to make a stronger unit.

Living, feeding or hunting in a group can help to keep animals safe. Many of them go for strength in numbers.

⇩ *Only a desperate predator would attack these wildebeest. They are alert and ready for action.*

Wily wildebeest

Wildebeest live in herds on the plains of Africa. They are hunted by predators such as lions and **hyenas**. Members of the herd work together to look out for predators and protect each other's youngsters. If threatened, their best defence is to give a powerful kick before running away.

⇧ A piranha fish shows off its razor-sharp teeth.

⇨ Piranhas hunt in groups. Here, a shoal of piranhas eats its prey alive.

Ferocious fish

One piranha fish on its own is not a powerful predator. But a shoal of piranhas is a force to be reckoned with. They are the most ferocious of all freshwater fish. Working together to rip at flesh, they can devour large mammals in a short time.

ACTUAL «« SIZE »»

Naked mole rat

Naked mole rats live in huge family groups of up to 250 individuals. Working like an army, they sometimes invade the tunnels of their neighbours, steal their young and force them to become workers, with the job of digging new tunnels to find food.

1 2 3 4 5 6 7 8 9 10
cm

Build it Up

A home can provide security, safety and a tough barrier to the outside world.

Many animals – both weak and strong – build homes to protect themselves and their families from predators and the weather.

Dog town

Black-tailed prairie dogs live together in enormous groups. Their underground burrows and tunnels, called towns, provide safety and warmth, especially at night and in the winter.

⬇ *A prairie dog emerges from its burrow to feed on grass and seeds.*

Paper houses

Paper is a lightweight material, but it can be very strong, and wasps use it to make their nests. They make the paper from wood pulp, which they chew and mould into the right shape. Each paper nest is home to the queen wasp and her growing eggs and **grubs**.

⇨ *This nest made by paper wasps protects the weak youngsters from predators, such as other insects, birds and small mammals.*

ACTUAL « SIZE »

Hermit crab

Hermit crabs have a shell, or carapace, that provides them with some strength, but these little crustaceans like extra security. When they find an empty seashell, they sneak inside and set up home.

1 2 3 4 5 6 7 8 9 10 11 12 13
cm

Moments of Weakness

Even strong animals sometimes struggle to survive the most difficult situations.

The no. 1 weakest baby **RECORD BREAKER** is the ...

RED KANGAROO

The largest kangaroos in the world are red kangaroos, which grow to 1.6 metres tall. As babies, however, they weigh less than one gram, and are so weak they have to be protected inside their mother's pouch while they grow bigger.

Some animals have developed clever ways to get through their moments of weakness.

Surviving winter

Winter weather can be one of the hardest challenges an animal has to face. One way to cope is to enter a time of deep sleep, or hibernation. By resting in a den, a bear can avoid the winter's bitter cold weather, frozen water and lack of food.

⇐ *A thirsty bear will roll snow in its paws to melt it.*

➡ *Periodical cicadas make a sudden and colourful appearance. Thousands of them emerge at the same time.*

Life change

Many insects go through big changes, called **metamorphoses**, when they change from egg to **larva** to adult. Larvae are often weaker than adults. Larvae of the periodical cicada are soft-bodied and have no defence systems, so they stay underground for about 17 years while they grow.

➡ *This periodical cicada larva is preparing for its final metamorphosis into an adult. Once it is an adult, it will eat very little, or nothing at all.*

Glossary

Antarctic The large continent that surrounds the South Pole.

Arctic The region that surrounds the North Pole. A large part of the Arctic region is a frozen sea.

Bird of prey A type of bird that attacks and eats smaller animals, such as rats, frogs and birds.

Crustacean An animal with a tough outer shell. Most crustaceans live in the sea.

Fungus A fungus is a living thing that is neither an animal nor a plant. Fungi feed on dead things. Mould and mushrooms are fungi.

Grub A young insect with a soft body is sometimes called a grub.

Hibernation The time during cold winter months that an animal spends resting and inactive.

Hyena An African predator that scavenges – it eats food left behind by other predators.

Larva A young insect, at a stage in its life before it becomes an adult with a different-shaped body.

Mammal An animal that has fur and feeds its young with milk.

Metamorphosis A complete change in body shape. Some insects change their body shape several times as they grow older.

Mineral A hard substance found in rocks. Living things need certain minerals to survive.

Ocean current An ocean current is a body of water in an ocean that is always flowing, like a river. Some currents flow near the surface, and others move deep underwater. They move heat around the world.

Plumage A bird's feathers are described as its plumage.

Pup A pup is the name given to the young of dogs and seals.

Tadpole Young frogs, toads and newts are called tadpoles. Tadpoles start without legs, but grow them as they get older.

Index

31

Notes for Parents and Teachers

Here are some ideas for activities that adults and children can do together.

◆ Before you read this book together, ask children for some examples of strong and weak animals. Talk about how they chose their examples, and what they think the words 'strong' and 'weak' mean. Revisit these ideas after reading the book, and talk about how the book might have changed their mind.

◆ Ask children to create a colourful poster of their five favourite strong animals. Help them decide how they should rank their chosen animals from one to five.

◆ Go through the book together and discover the meanings of any new words, using the glossary or a dictionary.

◆ The 'Actual Size' panels will help children understand many of the measurements mentioned in the book, but others need to be seen to be believed. Use a tape measure to explore some of the larger sizes quoted.

◆ Watch wildlife in gardens and parks, and talk about how different animals protect themselves from predators. A trip to a zoo or wildlife park will provide more opportunities to explore this topic.